# The pet

GW01417905

Nat and Meg sit in the hut. Nat is a vet. Meg is too.

Ted is sick. He has
a bad leg.

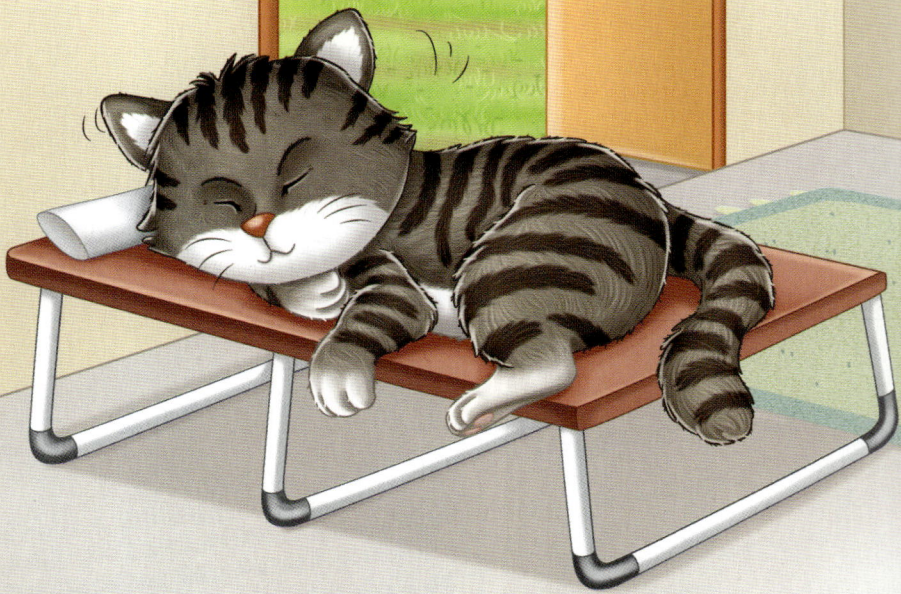

Sid is in the hut.
He naps on the bed.

Pam runs in.
She sits on the rug
and the bag.

Gus runs in, too.
He tugs at the rug.

Pet Vet

The hut is not big
and it is hot.

Nat and Meg cannot fit.
The pet vet is not for pets.

# Before reading

**Say the sounds:** c  k  ck  j  qu  v  w  x  y  z  zz  ff  ll  ss
Ensure the children use the pure sounds for the consonants without the added "uh" sound, e.g. "llll" not "luh".

**Practise blending the sounds:** vet  vets  sick  Meg  bed  hot  cannot  fit  leg  rug  bag  hut  tugs  naps  runs  bad  pet  pets  Ted  sits  sit  Gus  Pam  Nat  Sid  vet

**High-frequency words:** and  in  on  at  it  not  big  can
**Tricky words:** the  is  too  he  she  for  has

**Vocabulary check:** hut – What do the children think of when they think of a "hut"? What are some other words that can be used for a play space like that? (den, playhouse)

**Story discussion:** Look at the cover illustration and read the title. Which animals do you think might visit this pet vet?

**Teaching points:** Compare words like "runs" and "tugs", where the final "s" has a /z/ sound, with words like "vets" and "sits", where the final "s" has a /s/ sound.
Review two syllable and compound words, "cannot".

# After reading

**Comprehension:**
- What was wrong with Ted?
- What did Pam do in the hut?
- What did Gus and Sid do in the hut?
- Why did Nat and Meg send the pets out of the hut?

**Fluency:** Speed read the words again from the inside front cover.